Hymns in Concert

10 Late Intermediate to Early Advanced Piano Arrangements for Any Occasion

Judy East Wells

These hymn arrangements for late intermediate to early advanced levels are suitable for church services, hymn festivals or recitals. The variety of keys and moods in these arrangements makes them enjoyable for the performer as well as the listener.

All Creatures of Our God and King 4
How Firm a Foundation 13
I Need Thee Every Hour 18
It Is Well with My Soul 2
Like a River Glorious 6
My Faith Looks Up to Thee 20
O God, Our Help in Ages Past 8
O, How I Love Jesus 16
Softly and Tenderly/Lord, I'm Coming Home 22
There's a Land that Is Fairer Than Day 10

*This collection is dedicated to the memory of my grandmother,
Bettie Theresa Webb East,
who taught me a love for hymn playing.*

Cover illustration: Courtesy PhotoDisc

Copyright © MM by Alfred Publishing Co., Inc.
All rights reserved.   Printed in USA.
ISBN 0-7390-0916-8

All Creatures of Our God and King

Geistliche Kirchengesäng
Arr. by Judy East Wells

Like a River Glorious

James Mountain
Arr. by Judy East Wells

O God, Our Help in Ages Past

William Croft
Arr. by Judy East Wells

There's a Land that Is Fairer Than Day
(Sweet By and By)

Joseph P. Webster
Arr. by Judy East Wells

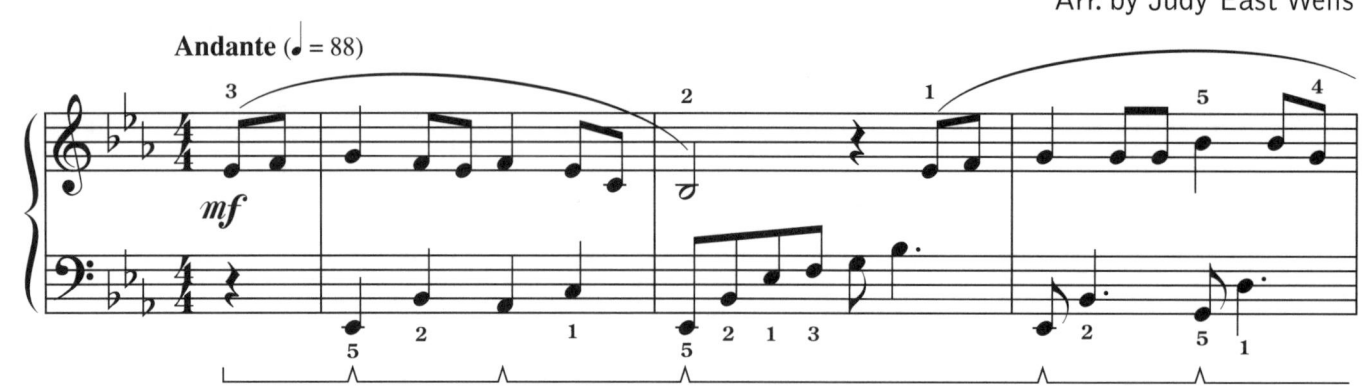

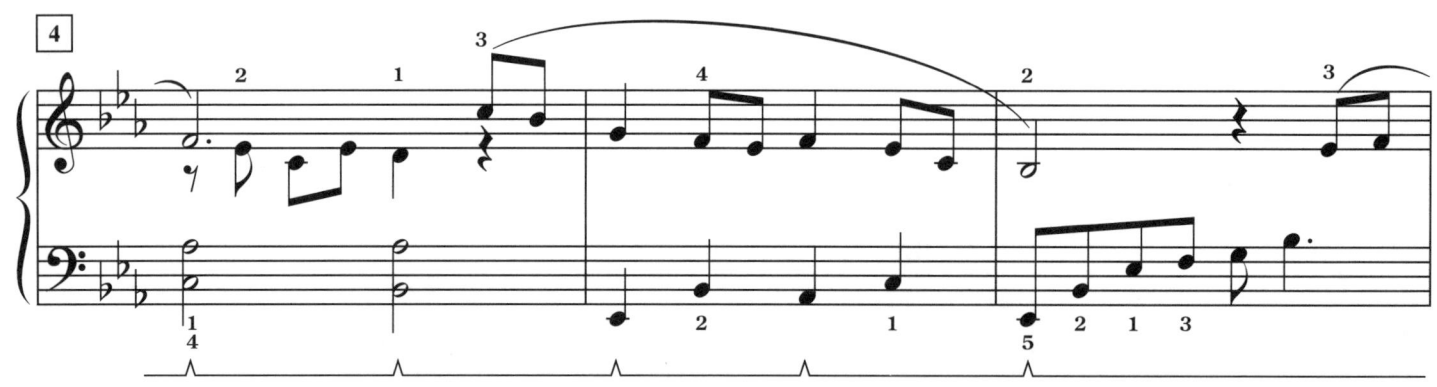

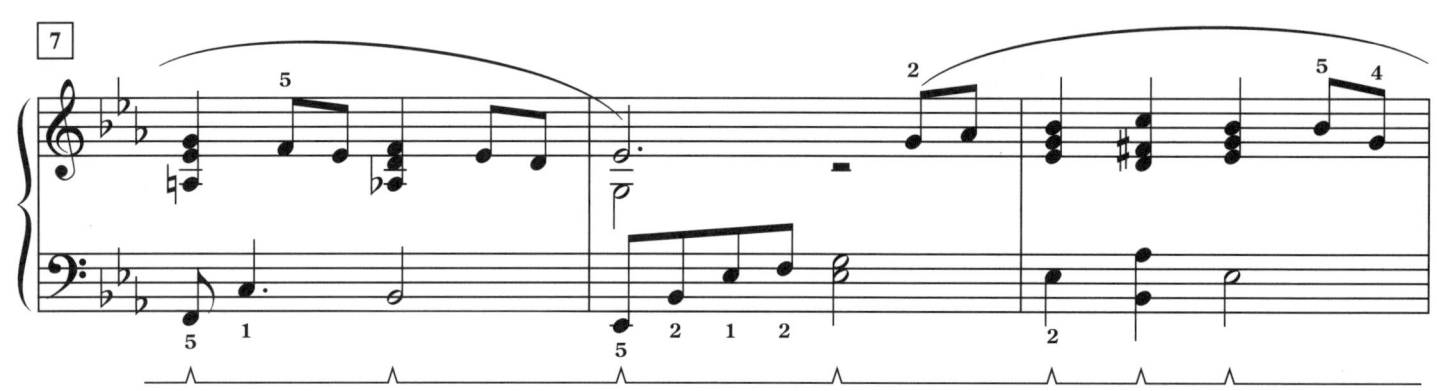

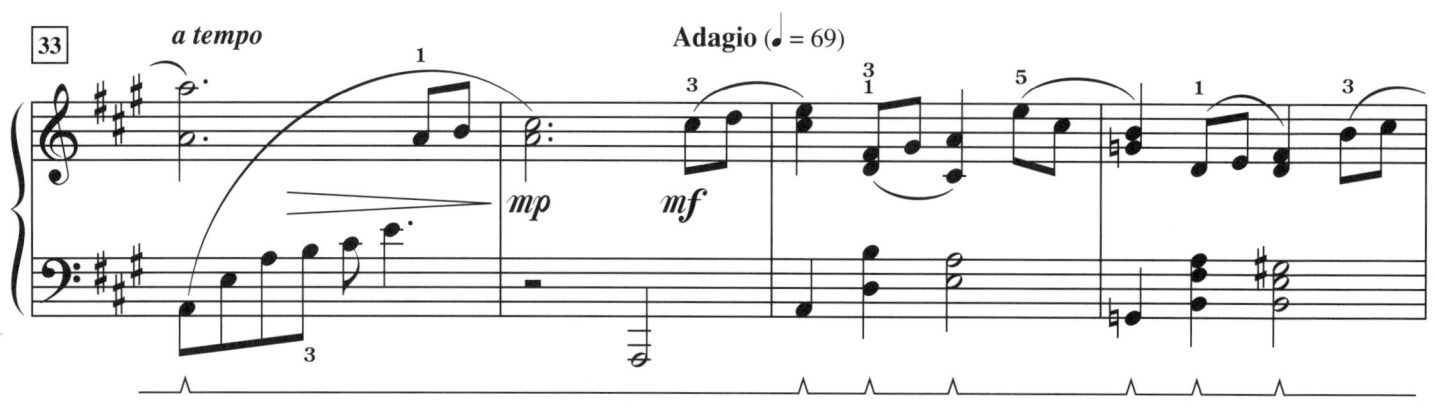

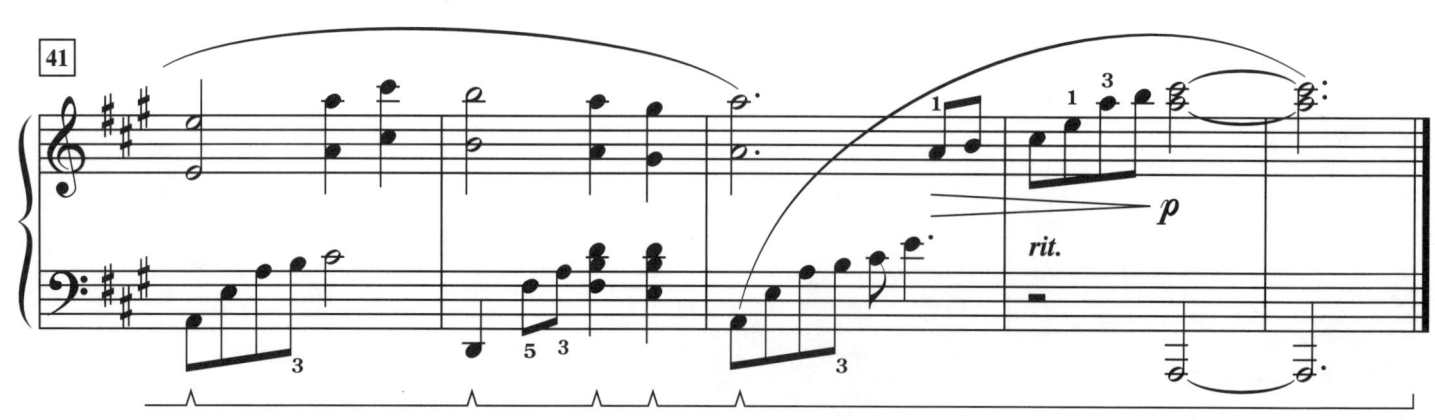

How Firm a Foundation

Early American melody
Arr. by Judy East Wells

O, How I Love Jesus

American melody
Arr. by Judy East Wells

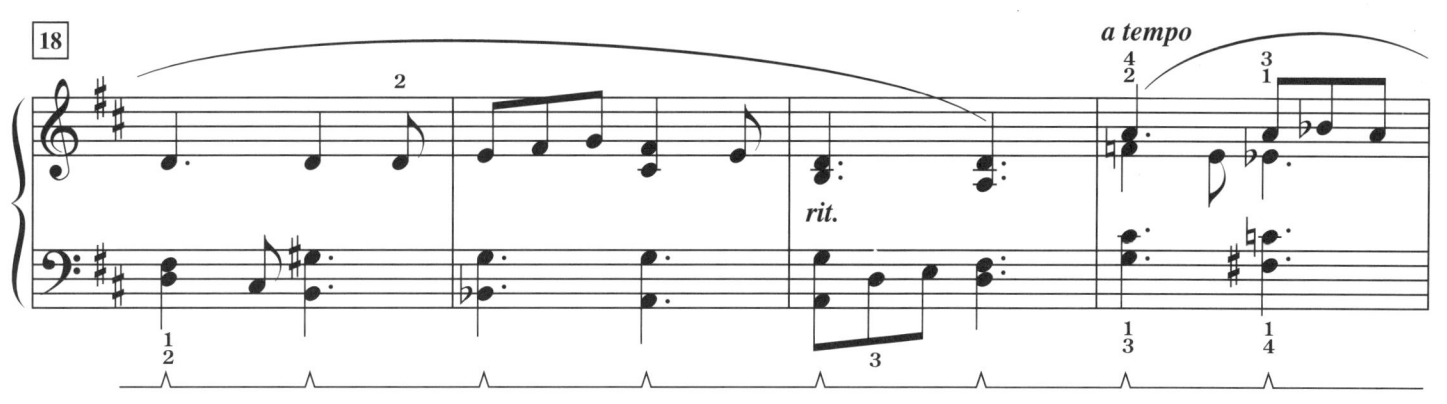

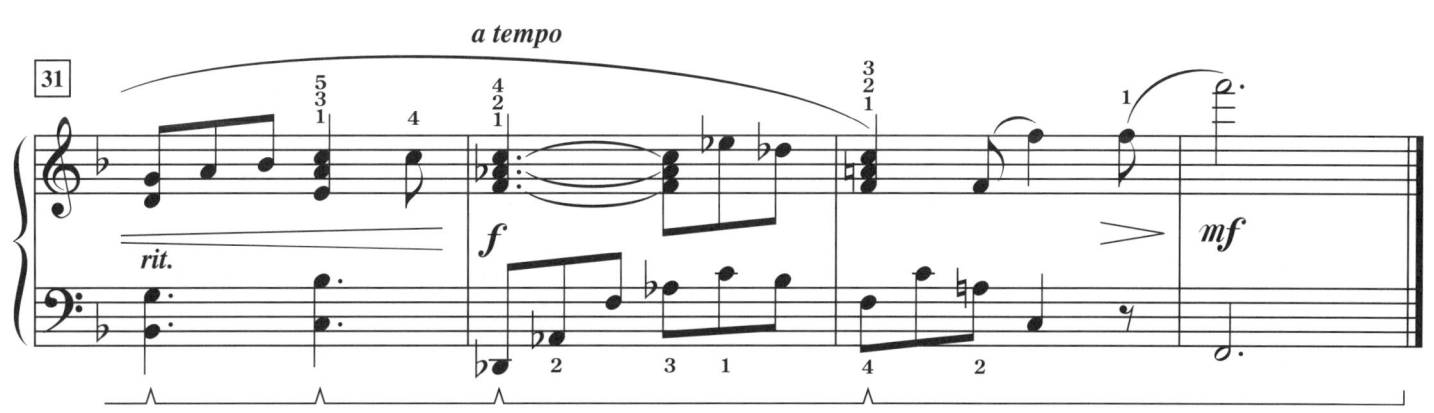

I Need Thee Every Hour

Robert Lowry
Arr. by Judy East Wells

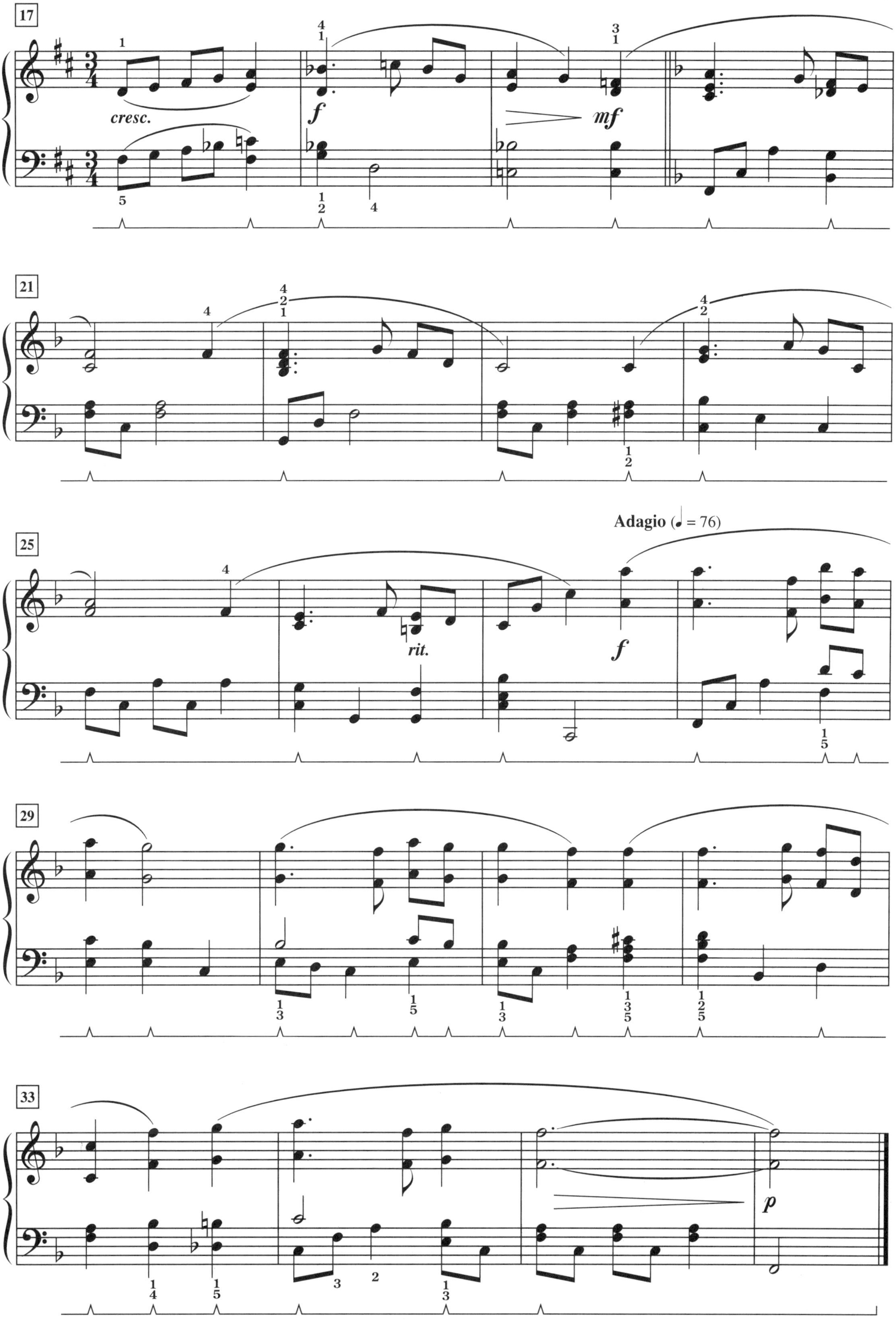
17
cresc.
f
mf
21
25
Adagio (♩ = 76)
rit.
f
29
33
p

My Faith Looks Up to Thee

Lowell Mason
Arr. by Judy East Wells

Softly and Tenderly / Lord, I'm Coming Home

Will L. Thompson/William J. Kirkpatrick
Arr. by Judy East Wells

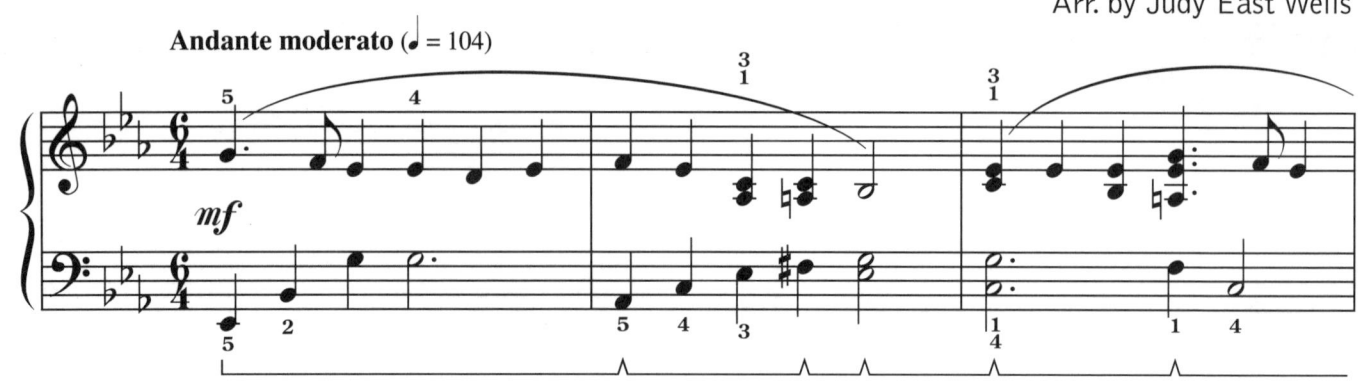

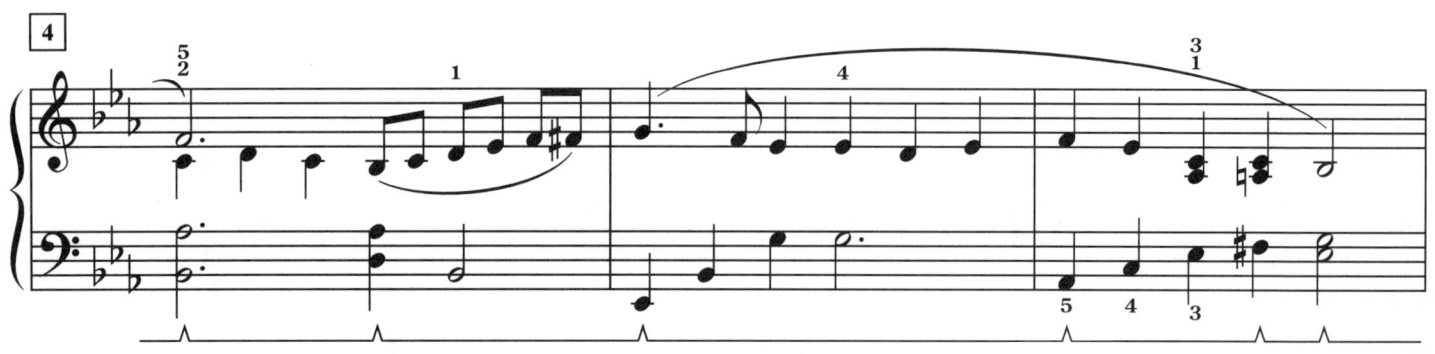

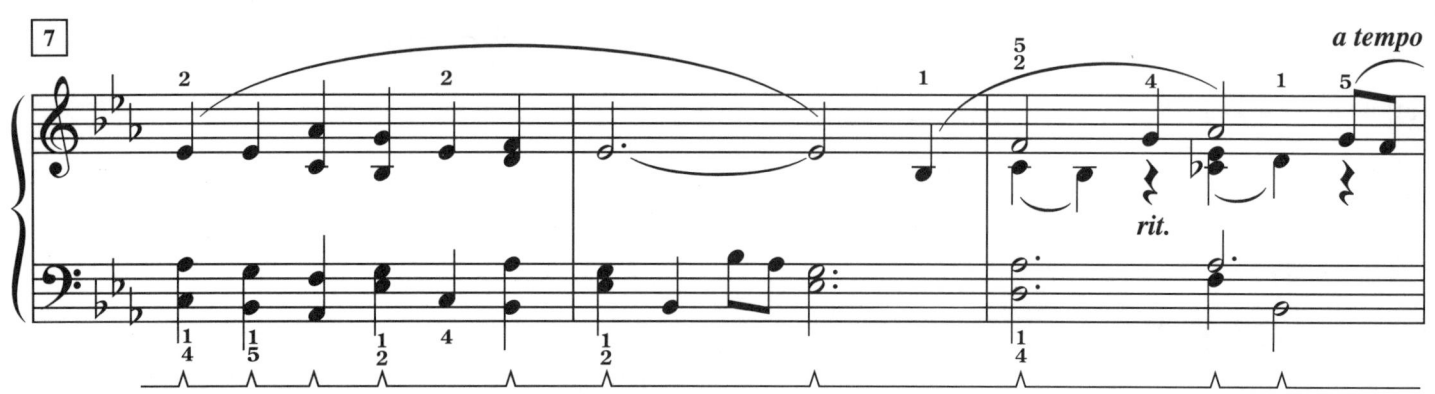

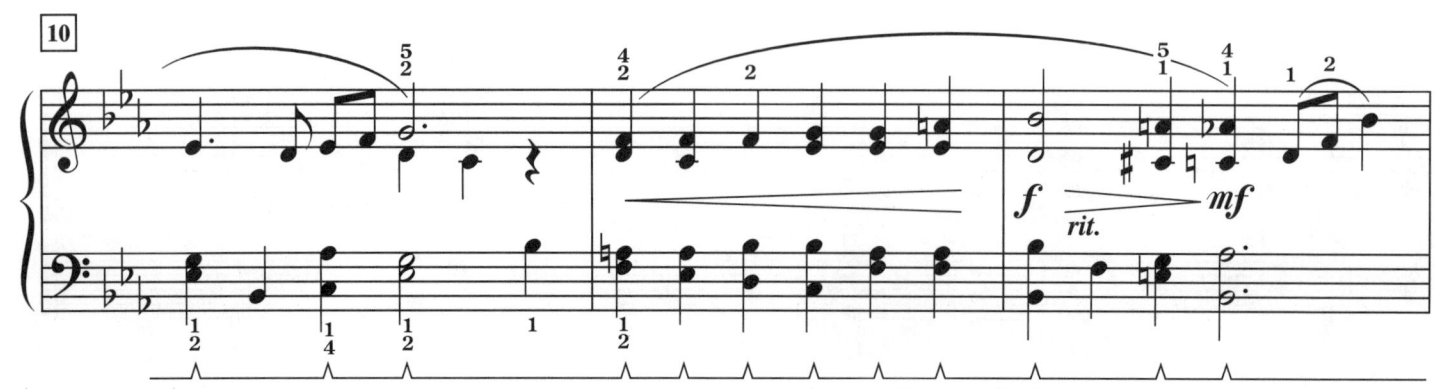

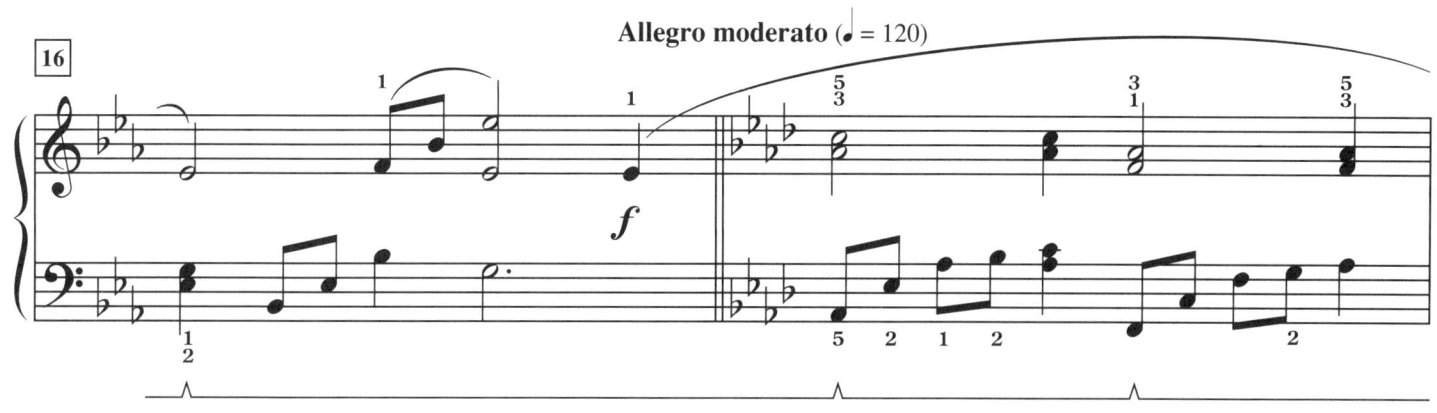
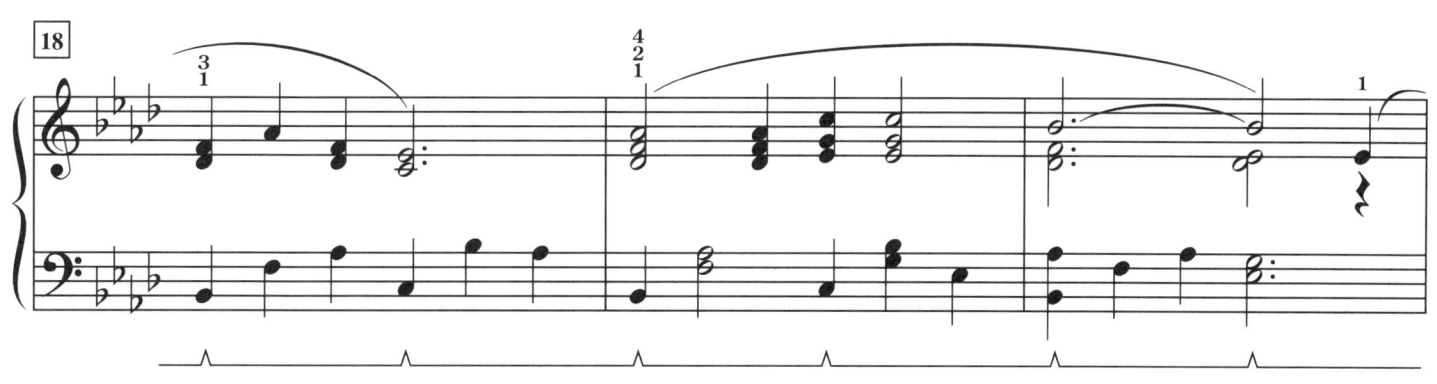
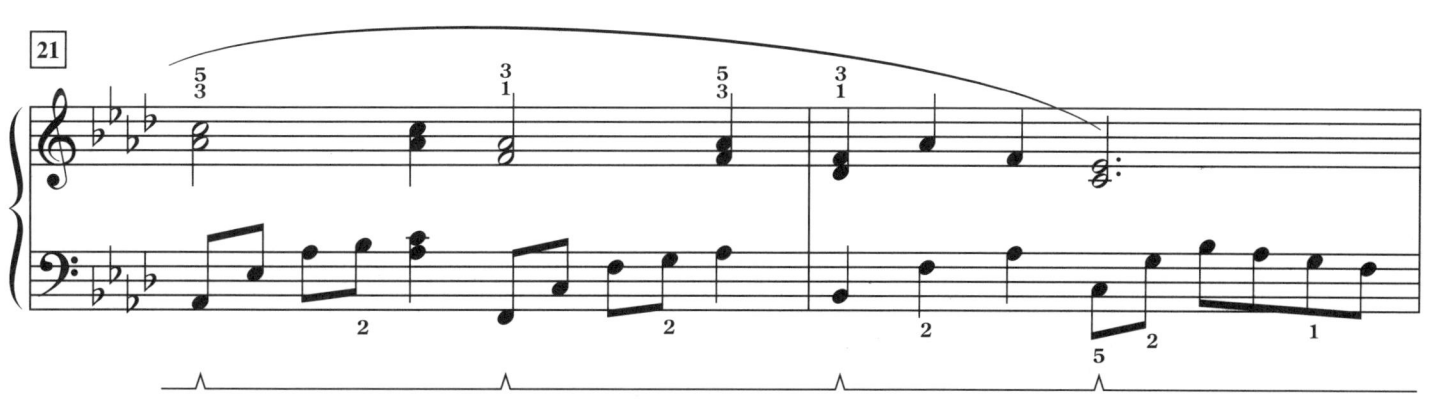

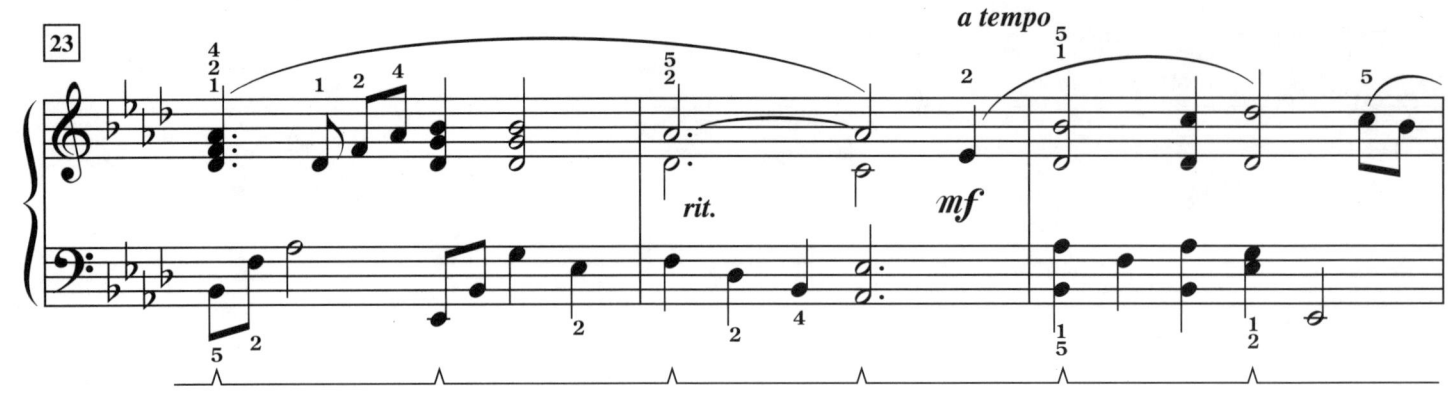
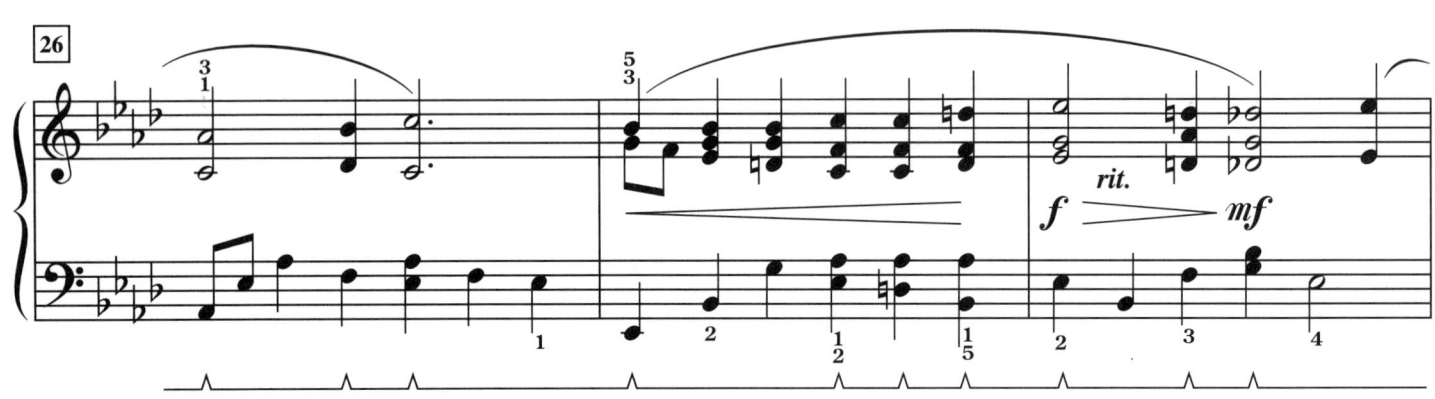

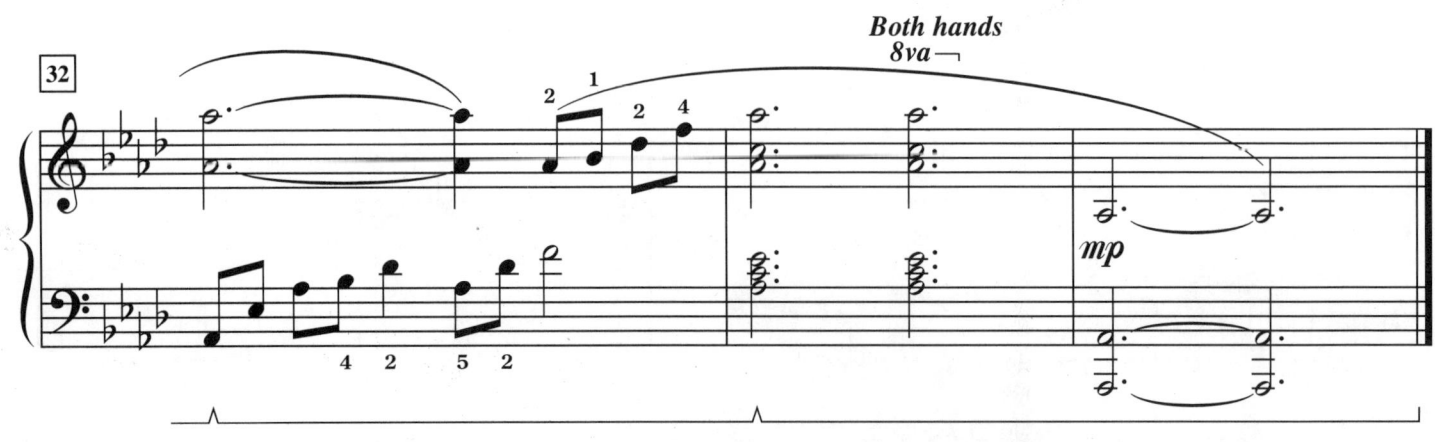